C000143282

MEDITERRANEO EDITIONS

Phaestos
Ayia Triada

Text by
STELLA KALOGERAKI
Archaeologist

Photographs / Layout
VANGELIS PAPIOMYTOGLOU

DTP
NATASSA ANTONAKI

Translation
JILL PITTINGER

Copyright 2004, 2012
MEDITERRANEO EDITIONS
36, Govatzidaki
74100 Rethymno, Crete, Greece
Tel. +30 28310 21590
Fax +30 28310 21591
e-mail: info@mediterraneo.gr
www.mediterraneo.gr

ISBN: 960-8227-37-2

Phaestos

Ayia Triada

CONTENTS

PHAESTOS

PHAESTOS OVER THE COURSE OF TIME   6
    Prepalatial period (2600 – 1900 BC)   8
    Old Palace period (1900-1700 BC)   9
    New Palace Period (1700-1450)   10
    Postpalatial and historic periods   11
A WALK AROUND THE PALACE   14
    The Upper Court   14
    The West Court and the Theatral area   15
    Circular constructions   16
    The façade of the Old Palace: the Shrine and the Propylaion   17
    The Façade of the Old Palace: Southern section   18
    The Monumental Staircase, the Propylaion of the
    New Palace and the areas around it   18
    The west magazine complex   21
    Passageway 18 and the rooms to the south of it   23
    The Central Court   25
    The east wing of the palace   28
    The north wing of the palace   29
    The Old Palace complex in the NE   33

AYIA TRIADA

AYIA TRIADA OVER THE COURSE OF TIME	36
A VISIT TO THE ARCHAEOLOGICAL SITE	37
The SE palace complex, the South Court, the Mycenaean Megaron and Stoa	37
The Neopalatial villa	39
The SW servants' complex	39
The NW royal apartments	40
The north magazines	42
The splendid NE complex	44
The north court, the 'bastion', the 'Mycenaean village', and the Mycenaean 'agora'	46

PHAESTOS

The palace of Phaestos was built on a hill which controls the whole plain of the Mesara, the largest and most fertile plain on Crete, from one end to the other. With a total area of 8,400 sq. metres it is the second most important palace of the Minoan world after Knossos and one of the four grand palaces of Crete. The view from it is truly panoramic; the Lasithi Mountains and Dikti rise up to the east, the Asterousia Mountains to the south, and Psiloritis to the north.

The Yeropotamos river, the famous Lethe of antiquity, flows along the northern and eastern sides of the hill, providing abundant water which covered all the requirements of the palace. Just as the whole area of the plain, the hill was already inhabited from the Late Neolithic period onwards; occupation continued without a break, reaching its high point during the 3rd and 2nd millennia B.C.
The name 'Phaestos' is met as 'Paito' on Linear B tablets from Knossos; it derives etymologically from 'phaestos', meaning 'shining, brilliant'. It is mentioned as one of the most important cities of Crete by several historians, among them Diodorus (5, 78) and Strabo (10, 479, 14), who believed that it had been founded by Minos himself. A more enduring belief was that held by Stefanos Byzantios, according to which the founder of the city was Phaestos, the grandson of Herakles (however, according to Pausanias II, 6, 6 he was the son

The first archaeological investigations by the Italian Archaeological School.

of Herakles). Referring to Phaestos, Homer states that it took part in the Trojan War; he describes it as a 'well-populated' city.

The first to arrive there in the mid-19th century was the English traveller, Captain H. Spratt, who identified the location as the ancient city of Phaestos and in referring to the hill of Kastri (II, 24) spoke of a locality which was completely bare and without any greenery at all.

The Palace of Phaestos came to light during excavations conducted by the Italian Archaeological School in 1900, immediately after the proclamation of the 'Cretan State'. The first head of the School was the archaeologist Federico Halbherr, who was subsequently succeeded by Luigi Pernier and after the Second World War, by Doro Levi.

The remains of two palaces were discovered; the older one was built around 1900 BC and destroyed around 1700 BC, and the new palace was built immediately after the destruction of the older one in 1700 and lasted until around 1450 B.C. Today, parts of both palaces are visible, a fact which often presents archaeologists with difficulties where interpretation is concerned.

The hill of Phaestos with the archaeological site, as seen from the west. The plain of the Mesara spreads out towards the east, 45 kms away, with the Lasithi Mountains in the background, while the foreground is dominated by the Church of Ayios Yeoryios of Falandra, which was dedicated to the Virgin during the Venetian period as a Catholic monastery.

PHAESTOS OVER THE COURSE OF TIME

Prepalatial period (2600 - 1900 BC)

During the 3rd millennium, around 2600 BC, the arrival of new racial elements combined with the use of bronze and precious metals led to the development of a new culture which gradually replaced the Neolithic and laid the foundations for the evolution of a glorious civilization which was later named Minoan. According to anthropologists, the new racial groups which arrived at the beginning of the period and blended with the Neolithic population of the island were of the Mediterranean type, although their exact origin cannot be determined.

The years from 2600 to 2000 BC constitute the Prepalatial period which divides into three phases: first, second and third. In the first phase the improvement of tools with the simultaneous use of those made from both bronze and stone, led to the development of agriculture, while the demand for tin which would harden bronze led to the development of seafaring and trade. These were the prerequisites which produced the brilliant civilization of the second phase of the Prepalatial period (2400-2100 BC) with its settlements and large houses, the appearance of the first tholos tombs, clay vessels which were now wheel-thrown, the

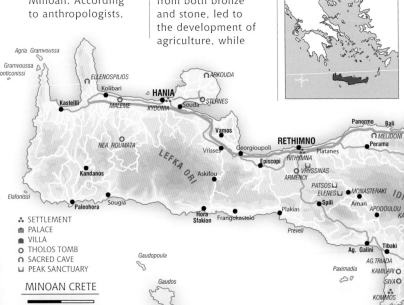

- ⁂ SETTLEMENT
- ⋔ PALACE
- ◼ VILLA
- ○ THOLOS TOMB
- ⋂ SACRED CAVE
- ⊔ PEAK SANCTUARY

MINOAN CRETE

wonderful metalwork, and in particular the jewellery of the highest workmanship and aesthetic. The third phase (2100-1900 BC) began with the sudden destruction of many settlements which were either abandoned or rebuilt in a much simpler way. Now, the first settlements appeared at Knossos, Phaestos, Malia and Zakros on sites which would later be levelled in order to build the first palaces. The tholos tombs, the most important of which have been discovered on the Mesara plain, continued in existence and were often enhanced by the addition of burial enclosures. The Goddess of fertility, otherwise the 'great Mother Goddess', continued to be worshipped and the first built elements appeared in the peak sanctuaries.

Old Palace period (1900-1700 BC)

With the beginning of the 2nd millennium and following a series of great upheavals in the Helladic area and the destruction of important centres in mainland Greece (Lefkandi, Lerna), a population explosion occurred. Mainly in the central and eastern part of Crete, the old settlements were enlarged and new ones were founded at the same time. Most important of all, real cities now appeared. The old palaces of Knossos, Phaestos, Malia and Zakros were built at the beginning of the Middle Minoan period (MM 1A). The birth of the system of palaces in Crete is either considered to be the result of cultural development from the settlements of the preceding period, or it is interpreted as a result of the developments

Pithos of the Old Palace period

of contacts with countries in the East. Centred on each of these palaces, territories were developed; their boundaries can be discerned on the basis of the radius of trade in the products which were manufactured in the workshops of the individual palaces. These cities remained unfortified, a fact which demonstrates the peaceful relations between them, while the discovery of archives with inscribed tablets and seals, as at Knossos, Phaestos, Malia and the building complex at Monastiraki Amariou, attest to the existence of an advanced system of

administration and economic control. During the Old Palace period, that is from 1900 to 1700, the palaces were destroyed three times. After the first and second destructions they were rebuilt on the same sites. However, after the third destruction in 1700, it was judged necessary to level the site and build the new palaces at higher levels.

Even though our knowledge about the first palaces is limited because they were destroyed and new ones built on their sites, we are in a position to be able to say that all were organized around a rectangular, central court, consisting of two or three storeys, magazines, complexes of rooms, sacred spaces, monumental entrances, and baths; they had an advanced water supply system and drainage.

The first palace of Phaestos which, like the other palatial centres on Crete, was built around 2000 BC and destroyed by an earthquake in 1700 BC, remains the best-preserved example of Old Palace period architecture on the island, in that its western part has been preserved.

New Palace Period (1700-1450)

The total destruction of the old palatial centres which occurred around 1700 BC was connected with seismic activity rather than with population incursions. The rebuilding which began immediately and continued for a period of around thirty years was aimed at the construction of palaces in exactly the same locations; now they were to be even more magnificent. We are fortunate; these palaces may have been destroyed, but new ones were not built on top of them. Thus, after the great discoveries at the beginning of the 20th century and the on-going research that has followed, we are able to gain an almost complete picture of the life and culture of this period.

New, grand palaces with huge areas were built again at Knossos, Phaestos, Malia and Zakros; new complexes were added at Ayia Triada and Archanes. In addition, the countryside was enriched with agricultural villa complexes which probably belonged to some kind of local leader. Such country villas have been found all over the island from Nerokourou near Hania, to Sklavokampos, Nirou Hani and Myrtos in central Crete and Sitia, Zou and Epano Zakros in eastern Crete. The architecture of the palatial complexes is the same in all of them, comprising a central and west court, light-wells, grandiose stairways, a propylaion, places for worship, magazines and numerous rooms. The second, magnificent palace which was built at Phaestos appears to be later in comparison to that of neighbouring Ayia Triada, which indicates that most probably, Ayia Triada and not Phaestos was the central residence of the local ruler.

Postpalatial and historic periods

After the second great destruction, habitation continued on the hill of Phaestos during the so-called postpalatial period, that is until the end of the Bronze Age. In historic times it continued in existence as a city, and an important one, as is evidenced by Homer who mentions it by name, and also by the archaeological remains dating from the Geometric and Archaic periods. The most notable amongst these is the Temple of Rhea, dating from the 7th century BC. As a great and independent city, Phaestos minted its own coinage, most of which bore the image of Europa sitting on a bull on one side and on the other the lion-headed Hermes sitting on a rock, or the Cretan giant Talos, or even Herakles with a lion. Although Phaestos was a great city with two harbours, at Matala and at Kommos, it could not withstand pressure from its neighbouring city of Gortys and was wiped out in 200 BC after a catastrophic attack by the forces of the latter.

PHASES OF THE PALACE
OF PHAESTOS

- PREPALATIAL
- OLD PALACE
- NEOPALATIAL
- POSTPALATIAL
- GEOMETRIC
- HELLENISTIC
- GREEK

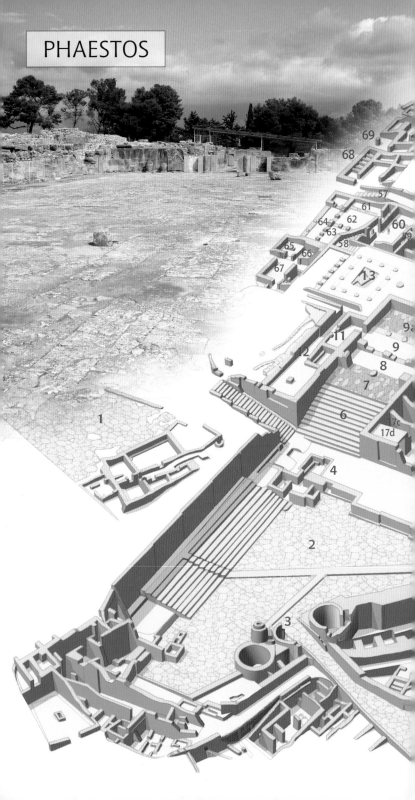

PHAESTOS

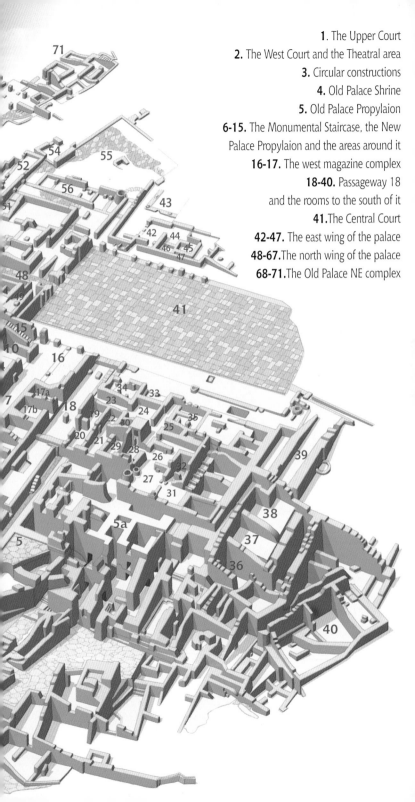

1. The Upper Court
2. The West Court and the Theatral area
3. Circular constructions
4. Old Palace Shrine
5. Old Palace Propylaion
6-15. The Monumental Staircase, the New Palace Propylaion and the areas around it
16-17. The west magazine complex
18-40. Passageway 18 and the rooms to the south of it
41. The Central Court
42-47. The east wing of the palace
48-67. The north wing of the palace
68-71. The Old Palace NE complex

A WALK AROUND THE PALACE

The Upper Court (1)

After arriving at the palace, the visitor first passes through the Upper Court, an open space in the northwest of the palace and on a higher level than the remaining areas. This court, which was already in existence in the first palace, was paved with irregular stones and is crossed in the east by a 'processional way', a raised path on a north-south orientation which was used for processions during cultic ceremonies.

The 17 round holes which can be seen on the western side were probably used for the placement of wooden columns which supported some kind of roof. The architectural remains on the southern side belong to buildings dating from the historic period. In one of these - a house on the southern side of the court - one room features a central hearth with two pillars, one on each side of it, as well as stone benches or seats around the walls. To the east of the court, elongated built structures have been discovered which probably belong to tombs of the Early Christian period.

The house on the west side of the upper court

View of the upper court, as seen from the north-west corner. The paving is visible, as is the 'processional way' and the remains of a house dating from the historical period on its south side.

The West Court and the Theatral area (2)

In the south-east corner of the Upper Court there is a stairway which leads to a lower level of the palatial complex, and in particular to the West Court. This stairway, which was originally thought to date from the Old Palace, has been proven to have been constructed along with the second palace. Thus, because the West Court belongs to the old palace, it seems that communication between it and the Upper Court must originally have been possible at some other location and not via the stairway just mentioned. The West Court, also paved with irregularly-shaped stones, is assigned as we have said to the

The west court, the central processional way and the theatral area on the northern side of the court.

Old Palace period, that is, it belonged to the first palace of Phaestos. It is crossed by two raised processional ways, the largest of which leads to nine wide steps and continues over them. The steps, which clearly did not belong to a stairway, are the 'tiers' of a theatral area and abutted the wall which supported the Upper Court. On its southern edge the large, oblique pathway turns eastwards in the direction of the central court. Generally, the open space of the west court, which is

The central processional way of the west court turns towards the east to continue on to the propylaion of the Old Palace and the central court.

really outside the palace complex, was designated for religious ceremonies and perhaps also for athletic contests. When the construction of the second palace took place the whole of the west court was filled in with

The stairway which leads from the upper court to the central court.

The West Court and the Theatral area

earth, covering the first five steps of the theatral area. Thus, a new floor was created at a higher level which facilitated the design of, and access to, the propylaion of the new palace.

Circular constructions (3)

The second pathway of the West Court, which in reality branches off from the first, leads to four circular constructions in the west of the court, two of which are only half-preserved. It is probable that these were used for grain storage. They are assigned chronologically to the period of the first palace.

One of the circular constructions in the south-western corner of the west court.

A circular construction in the south-west corner of the west court, which has been cut into by a later, paved way.

The façade dating from the Old Palace period : the Shrine (4) and the Propylaion (5)

Along the length of the eastern side of the West Court and at a lower level than that of the New Palace period façade, excavation has revealed the remnants of the façade of the old palace. Starting in the northern part of this façade a number of finds were made

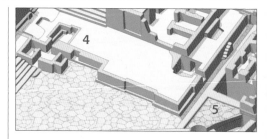

of a particular, characteristic nature, such as an 'offertory table' and a triton, which defined the use of this place as a Shrine. The latter comprised five covered areas and an open space. Three of the five rooms which extended in the direction of the West Court are ordered in such a way that they recall the 'tripartite shrines' which are well-known from Minoan art and religion. Also indicative of the cultic nature of

The west façade of the Old Palace of Phaestos, as seen from the West Court.

the place are the benches of stone which run around the walls of some of the rooms. Continuing further southwards there was a series of rooms, subsequently filled in, with the characteristics of stores and workshops. At its SW corner, the façade of the Old Palace turns eastwards in the direction of the central court. Immediately after it makes this turn there is the only known entrance to the Old Palace, in front of which there was the monumental propylaion of the Old Palace with its pillar in the middle (of which only the base

The SW corner of the northern part of the Old Palace façade.

is preserved). A little further to the east there is a storeroom containing pithoi which are still in situ;

this also dates from the period of the first palaces.

The northern part of the façade of the Old Palace. The rooms of the shrine can be seen exactly in front of the monumental stairway which leads to the interior of the New Palace.

The Façade of the Old Palace:
Southern section (5a)

To the south of the propylaion of the Old Palace with its monumental pillar, there is a series of rooms which also date from the Old Palace period. This complex, which is roofed over and inaccessible to the public, comprised mostly storerooms and places used for workshops; access was via the lower court.

Storeroom (magazine) of the Old Palace period, with pithoi preserved in situ; situated in the part of the archaeological site inaccessible to the general public.

The Monumental Staircase, the Propylaion of the New Palace and the areas around it (6-15)

Access to the New Palace was via a monumental staircase (6) which was situated in the NE corner of the west court. The staircase consists of 12, low steps which also led to the equally monumental Propylaion; it is probable that the stairway was used as a complement to the theatral area of the west court, which as we have said was limited to only four steps during the New Palace period because of the filling-in of the west court. The façade of the propylaion included a pillar which

The propylaion (7) with its characteristic pillar between two pilasters.

was set between two pilasters **(7)** and was thus divided into three parts. Today, only the base of this pillar is preserved; it was of huge dimensions and

The monumental entrance stairway (6) to the New Palace, situated at the NE corner of the west court.

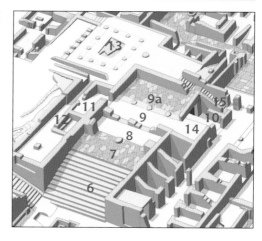

The triple magazine complex (10) dating from the Old Palace period.

A pithos in the Old Palace magazine (10).

The monumental entrance stairway dating from the New Palace period (6) with the west court and theatral area in front of it.

The triple colonnade which surrounded the light-well (9a) in the area of the propylaion.

Spaces 8 and 9 of the propylaion.

The magazine of the Old Palace (10), situated below the level of the New Palace light-well.

had an ellipsoid cross-section. After passing through the façade of the propylaion we reach an anteroom **(8)** which is noteworthy because of its alabaster floor and from there, two openings lead into a space with a triple colonnade **(9)** which is designated a light-well **(9a)**; below it, a three-roomed magazine **(10)**, dating from the Old Palace period, has been discovered. This magazine, in which about 30 pithoi were found still in situ, was filled in when the construction of the

The entrance to the stairway (11) to the north of the triple colonnade of the propylaion.

The stairway (15) which linked the light-well of the propylaion (9a) with the anteroom of the magazines (16)

The 'waiting room' (14) to the south of anteroom (9) of the light-well.

propylaion of the New Palace was undertaken. The propylaion complex afforded three possibilities for access to various parts of the palace. Exactly to the north of the triple colonnade (9), a stairway **(11)** ascended to a passageway **(12)** leading to a hypostyle hall **(13)**, through which there was access to the royal apartments. On the SE end of the eastern wall of the light-well (9a), there was an opening onto a stairway **(15)** which led to an anteroom of the magazines (16) and the central court (41). Finally, in the south wall of the space with the colonnade (9) there was an opening and a stairway which led to a room **(14)** known as the 'waiting room'. The nature of the room was defined by the built benches against the walls, where visitors to the palace were able to sit. Exactly below the waiting room (14) excavations revealed a lustral basin dating to the Old Palace period which indicates that during the period of the first palace this place was used for religious rites.

The passageway (12) leading to a hypostyle hall and the royal apartments.

The hypostyle hall (13), as seen from the SW corner.

The west magazine complex (16-17)

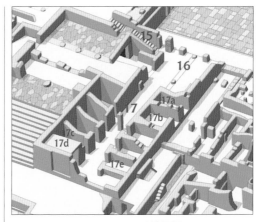

Following the stairway (15) which is situated in the SE corner of the light-well of the propylaion, we descend to the Anteroom of the Magazines **(16)**, the inside of which is characterized by two pillars. The floor is paved and exactly beneath it was found an archive of Old Palace sealstones. West of the anteroom there is the passage with the complex of magazines **(17)** to the left and right of it. Half-way along the passage the base of a rectangular pillar has been preserved; this probably served to support the floor

The floor of alabaster paving in the anteroom of the magazines (16).

above it. In the NW corner of the complex there is the magazine which is roofed over today **(17d)**, containing tall pithoi and a receptacle sunk into the floor to collect liquids. The room in the SE corner of the

Stairway 15 and the anteroom of the magazines (16)

The west magazine complex

Magazine 17c, with a collection of stone objects found in various parts of the archaeological site.

Stone vessels from various locations in the archaeological site which are gathered together in 17e, in the south wing of the magazine complex.

complex (17a) was not accessible from the long passage but from passage (18) and as we shall see below, apparently constituted some kind of porter's lodge, the purpose of which was to check on those passing along passageway 18 to the central court (41). There was the possibility of access from the anteroom (16) to the central court (41) via a monumental entrance which comprised a pillar between two support columns which would have reached to the height of the second storey of the magazines.

The anteroom of the magazines (16) and in the background the passage with the storerooms to the left and right of it (17).

A pithos in magazine 17d.

Magazine 17d which is roofed over today, in the NW corner of the magazine complex.

Passageway 18 and the rooms to the south of it (18-40)

To the south of the complex of magazines there is a passage **(18)** which has an east-west orientation, and connects the two large courts of the palace, the west and the central court. At its eastern end there is the base of a column which supported the floor above, while at the western end there are the remains of the propylaion of the Old Palace. It has been suggested that room **17a** was a guardroom and that **17b** provided access from the passage (18) to the magazine complex (17). Finds of a cultic nature, such as 'offertory tables' which came from rooms **19-22**, define the nature of these adjacent rooms as a shrine. Room 21, with its benches around the walls, yielded ritual vessels and cultic figurines, providing further evidence for the use of this complex. A little before the eastern end of passage 18 another passage **(23)** leads off in a southerly direction to a complex of rooms **(24-32)** which was most probably accessible at some earlier stage from the central court. Room **32** with its little descending staircase and room **30** with the pillar have been identified as 'lustral basins'. In general, we can say that this carefully-built complex (24-32) was also of a cultic character and was intended for the

The complex of rooms to the south of passage 18.

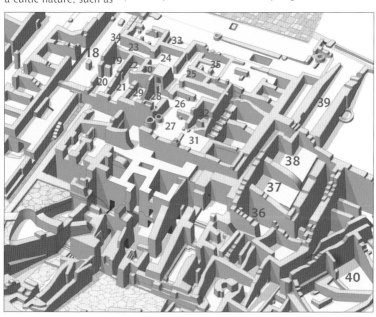

The rooms of the west wing which had access to the Central Court.

Passage 18 to the south of the magazine complex

Rooms 33 and 34 with the characteristic benches around the walls.

Room 34 with the benches and the little table.

The rooms of the west wing which had access to the Central Court.

carrying out of religious rites.

We are led via passage 18 to rooms **33-34** which face onto the central court (41) and are directly connected with it. Room **33** has benches and a pillar between two pilasters at its entrance. Similarly, room **34** has benches, an alabaster floor and a little clay 'table' in the middle. South of rooms 33-34 there is another space **(35)** of a cultic nature with a façade onto the central court. Its nature, even though it has undergone changes because of the later building constructed almost on top of it, is witnessed by the two column bases found inside it.

At the southern end of the west wing there are three more rooms **(36-38)**; they are in a bad state of

The remains of the archaic temple of Rhea (40).

preservation and their purpose cannot be determined. A huge retaining wall rises up in front of them and apparently constituted the southern boundary of the palace. Outside this wall, at a much later date and at an oblique orientation to that of the Minoan buildings, the archaic temple of Rhea or the Mother Goddess **(40)** was built; according to current theory she was the successor of the Minoan goddess of vegetation and fertility. To the east of the complex of three rooms 36-38 there was passage **39** with a floor of alabaster paving. The large drainage channel of the central court was located at its eastern end.

The large drainage channel found at the SW end of the Central Court.

The Central Court (41)

The Central Court of the palace, which was already paved from the Old Palace period, was re-used with the same floor during the New Palace period. Along its eastern and western sides there were porticos (stoas) which were formed by colonnades with pillars and columns placed alternately. It should be noted that during the New Palace period the court was extended towards the west; this is witnessed by a narrow strip without paving below the western portico. From the wall on the northern side with its recesses, projections, alcoves and half-pillars there was access to the royal apartments. All of the rooms and spaces

The northern façade of the central court (41).

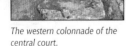

The western colonnade of the central court.

The eastern colonnade of the central court.

were linked via this court, which was the centre of the palace, even though it has to be said that access to the court was via narrow passageways with doors and a strict system of control, a fact which indicates that it was not a place open to all. The superb central court with its large dimensions was probably reserved for important rites, athletic events and perhaps even for bull-leaping. The stepped construction in the NW corner of the court may have been an altar, although this is not certain.

Stone channel below the paving of the central court at its SW end.

Pithoi at the northern façade of the central court 41.

One of the recesses in the northern façade of the central court.

A well, dating from a later period, in the central court.

The east wing of the palace (42-47)

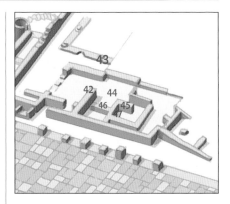

In the eastern part of the palatial complex, immediately behind the eastern colonnade of the central court, there is a group of particularly fine rooms. Entrance to them was from a point in the eastern portico (stoa), where there were four steps. The little stairway originally led to room **42** with its characteristic polythyro, a system of wooden openings which were supported by stone pilasters and meant that the room could be wide open or closed according to the temperature and prevailing weather conditions. To the east of this area with the polythyro (42) there is a portico **(43)** with a colonnade consisting of four columns arranged in the form of the Greek letter Γ.

Room 42 with the characteristic polythyro

To the south of the polythyro (42) there is an anteroom **(44)** which leads to a 'lustral basin' **(45)**, a place of cultic character which is attested by the numerous ritual objects which were found in it, such as double axes, rhyta, a pair of horns of consecration and many vessels. Immediately to the west of rooms 44 and 45 are rooms **46** and **47** whose purpose has not yet been determined.

Portico 43 east of room 42.

The luxurious construction of this eastern complex has led certain researchers to characterize it as the princely living quarters, although nothing definite has been established.

Rooms 44 and 45 of the eastern complex. To the west of them are the long, narrow rooms 46 and 47 whose purpose has not been ascertained.

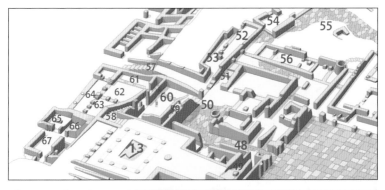

The north wing of the palace (48-67)

On the northern side of the central court there was the magnificent façade of the north wing of the palace, where the most impressive and luxurious rooms, including the royal apartments, were discovered.

About in the middle of the north side of the central court there was the doorway to a wide passage **(48)**. To the left and right of it there were two wooden half-pillars supported on wooden bases. Beside them were two alcoves decorated with wall-paintings, in which according to one view those guarding the wing were stationed. Entering the passage, there was another recess immediately on the left from which it would have been possible to guard the stairway **(49)**

The impressive entrance and the wide passage (48) which led to the royal apartments.

leading to the upper floor of the royal apartments which are not preserved today. To the right and left of the passage there are groups of rooms which must have existed from the period of the old palaces and were re-used. Some were decorated with wall-paintings, and a feature of one of these rooms is constituted by the 'cupboards' built into the walls. Passage 48 ends at a doorway which leads to the court **(50)** with the round cistern dating from the historic period and the paved floor of the Old

The recess to the left of the entrance of passage 48.

Palace beneath that of the new palace. In the NE corner of the court (50) there is an exit into a passage **(51)**. The latter runs eastwards and must have provided access to room **52** which had a paved floor. This room had been built partly above room

The north wing of the palace

The stairway (49) which led to the upper floor of the royal apartments.

The paved court 50 with the round cistern.

The eastern court 55. The workshops (56) can be seen on the right.

53 of the Old Palace which in view of the finds made there, has been designated a 'lustral basin'. In its continuation, passage 51 passed a small room **(54)** with a bench and an alabaster floor which has been characterized as a porter's lodge and ended at the east court **(55)** which was also paved; the remains of a horseshoe-shaped oven made of clay have been found in the middle of it. Along the western side of this court there is a series of 6 small rooms **(56)** which have been assigned a direct association with the oven and for this reason have been designated as workshops.

The series of six 'workshops' to the west of the eastern court, as seen from the north.

We return to court 50 and follow the open-air passage **57** which leads to the **royal apartments**, although the exact point of access to them is not discernible today. It is most probable however, that entrance was only effected from the first floor via the stairways **58** and **59**, and the possibility that passage 57 was connected to stairway 59 by means of an accessory wooden stairway, which naturally no longer exists today, cannot be excluded.

Royal apartments. The portico (64) in front of rooms 62 and 63 with the characteristic polythyro.

The luxurious apartments are notable for their alabaster floors, wall-paintings, light-wells and advanced drainage system; they are by no means second to those at the palace of Knossos or the magnificent complex of Ayia Triada.

Room **60** divides into three sections with two pairs of pillars placed parallel to each other, permitting the formation of a light-well and leaving the middle section of the room open to the sky. The walls of the whole apartment were lined with sheets of alabaster and the western part, in addition to the alabaster dado, also had a floor of alabaster paving, benches and wonderful wall-paintings with rosettes. In the NW corner of the room there was a stairway (59) with two branches which led to the upper floor. This luxurious apartment is thought to have been that of the queen. Via an impressive pillared opening on the northern side of the room there was communication with stairway 58 which ascended to the peristyle court **13**; the latter constituted part

Room 60 of the royal apartments, with the polythyro, portico and light-well.

of the second floor of the royal apartments. The colonnade on four sides, consisting of four pillars on each of the sides, formed a surrounding portico with an alabaster floor and left the central part of it uncovered; in the middle of this area a room dating from the prepalatial period has been discovered. In the northern part of this area there was a polythyro with six openings; a little staircase to the south of the court connected it with the propylaion (9) and the monumental entrance to the palace (6).

We return to stairway 58, in order to descend to the royal apartments on the lower floor (61, 62, 63, 64). In room **63** there is a polythyro with four openings on its northern and four on its eastern side.

Royal apartments. Anteroom 65 and lustral basin 66.

Immediately to the east of 63 lies room **62** with a double opening in the north formed by a column between two pilasters. The more easterly room **(61)** is an open-air light-well, as is demonstrated by its floor which here is made of lime, as opposed to the alabaster of the two previous rooms. North of rooms 62 and 63 there is a portico **(64)** consisting of three pillars. This portico is situated between two small rooms which project from its northern façade.

The more northerly of the two rooms has been characterized as a 'guardroom'. In the SW corner of the area with the polythyro (63) there is an opening onto a passage which leads to the anteroom of a lustral basin **(65)** and from there, via a stairway with seven steps, to the lustral basin itself **(66)**. Room 67, which could be accessed from the anteroom of the lustral basin (65) has been characterized as a 'toilet', because of the system of drains which criss-crossed its floor.

The passage leading to anteroom 65 and lustral basin 66.

The Old Palace complex in the NE (68-71)

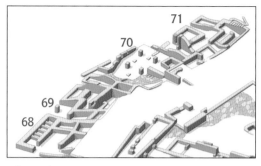

All of the buildings which have been uncovered on the NE slope of the hill of Phaestos have been dated to the Old Palace period, even though it is certain that they were re-used during the period of the new palaces. Although it is isolated, there is no doubt that this complex was connected to the rest of the palace by a stairway which linked room **(70)** with the eastern court. Access can be gained to the buildings in the NE if we begin from the central court, follow passage 48 which leads to court 50 and from there proceed along passage 57, and go down the wooden stairway to arrive at building **68**. Here, a series of brick partitions

formed repositories where excavations have revealed that cultic and other precious objects were kept. Here, the famous Phaestos disk was discovered in

1908, and dated to the beginning of the New Palace period (1700-1600 BC). It is a clay disk with hieroglyphs stamped on both sides and depicting human

The **Phaestos Disk**. This clay disk was found in a place where valuable objects were stored in the NE complex of the palace (68). The spiral inscription contains symbols placed in groups between incised lines. Although many attempts have been made to decipher it, we are not in a position to know the contents of the text.
Archaeological Museum of Heraklion.

The storage repositories (68) in the NE complex of the palace. The Phaestos Disk was found in one of them.

The Old Palace complex in the NE

figures, vessels, tools, plants, animals, birds etc. There is a total of 241 signs of 45 different types. The signs are arranged within a spiral, organized in groups which are divided off from each other by vertical lines, probably forming words. This find, which is undoubtedly Cretan, appears to be of religious significance.

The adjacent building **(69)** is characterized by a pillar in its northern façade, which probably gives it a cultic nature although some researchers have considered

The private dwelling 70 with the peristyle court.

that it served as a guardhouse for the one next to it; a passage led from it to complex **70**. The latter appears to have been a private, two-storeyed dwelling with an internal peristyle court which was linked to the central

palace complex via a stairway on its southern side. Finally, the more easterly complex of rooms **(71)** was designated a 'potter's storeroom', because a large number of unused vessels was found there.

Clay krater in Kamares style, decorated with flowers 'in relief'. Old Palace period, Archaeological Museum of Heraklion.

A clay jug, its whole surface decorated with a leaf design. It is assigned to the floral style and dated to the end of the New Palace period. Archaeological Museum of Heraklion.

AYIA TRIADA

Three kilometers to the west of Phaestos there was the Venetian village of Ayia Triada, of which only two churches of the 14th century have been preserved: the double-aisled Church of Ayia Triada (Holy Trinity) and the Church of Ayios Yeoryios Galatas inside the archaeological area. The site, which was uncovered to the east of the medieval village, took its name from the Church of Ayia Triada. The Minoan royal villa or small palace began to come to light at the beginning of the 20th century, when the Italian Archaeological School arrived in the area, first under the leadership of Federico Halbherr and then under Luigi Pernier. It has been determined that there was already a settlement dating from the Neolithic period on the hill on which the villa was situated, although the remains visible today date mainly from the New Palace and Mycenean periods. It is certain that the construction of the complex began not only after the destruction of the old palaces, but after the completion of the new palace of Phaestos, with which it must have had close connections. The so-called 'villa', which must have been built around 1550 BC and was destroyed by the fires connected with the earthquakes which rocked Crete in 1450 BC (thus its life was only one of about 100 years) probably constituted the summer residence of the illustrious officials of the central and undisputed palace of Phaestos.

After the great catastrophe of 1450 BC a long period of time passed, roughly down to the Mycenean period, before buildings were constructed again on the site, on top of the ruins of the New Palace period. The architectural remains from the period 1380-1100 BC are well-preserved and provide important information about this period on Crete.

Scant remains from the historic period bear witness to the fact that during the Geometric, Archaic and Classical periods life continued in the area, which now functioned mainly as a place for worship. It was known as such during the Hellenistic period, when a temple was built there and dedicated to Zeus Velchanos.

Federico Halbherr, director of the Italian Archaeological School, which brought to light the archaological site of Ayia Triada in 1902.

7d
7h
7i
7c
7e
7f
7b
7a 6d
6a
6c

A VISIT TO THE ARCHAEOLOGICAL SITE

The SE palace complex, the South Court, the Mycenaean Megaron and Stoa

After we enter the archaeological site from the south, the SE complex of the palace is spread out exactly on our left. This comprises a large number of rooms, perhaps an independent dwelling of the New Palace period, in the western tract of which there were magazines **(1)** and in the eastern tract two adjacent colonnades **(2a, 2b)** and a stairway which led to the upper floor. Although the dwelling gives the impression that it must have taken the form of a Greek letter Π with an internal court, the scant remains of walls which have been discovered demonstrate that this area must have been filled with rooms. To the SE of the house, a shrine was built during the Mycenaean period **(3)**. The shrine, which was entered from the west, consisted of an anteroom and main inner recess which was entered through a double pilastered opening. In addition to a stone bench, the latter had a floor decorated with marine frescoes. The shrine

NORTHERN ROAD

SOUTH COURT

NEOPALATIAL

MYCENAEAN

LATER

The SE complex, as seen on the left by the visitor when entering the site.

(3) constituted part of the so-called 'Court of Shrines', an open-air sanctuary which developed in the area of the southern court of the villa and the later Mycenean megaron, towards the end of the Bronze Age.

The south court of the Neopalatial villa was paved and covered with new paving again during the Mycenaean period, at the time when the magnificent megaron ($4^a4^b4^c4^d$) was built on top of it, covering a large area of the villa, and particularly its southern façade, with its massive foundations. The megaron was rectangular in form, separated into three sections; on its southern side there was a portico with a colonnade, from which the bases of three columns are preserved. Further to the south of the portico, a stairway with five steps ascended in the direction of the cemetery of the Church of Ayios Yeoryios Galatas. A paved roadway with drainage channels ran from the east of the

The 'Court of Shrines' situated in the southern court of the villa. Part of the magazine area (1) of the SE complex can be seen in the foreground.

megaron, while further east there was a stoa (5^a5^b) which also dates from the Mycenaean period. The finds from the stoa, among which are the stone bases of double axes which are housed today in the Archaeological Museum of Heraklion, indicate that it must have been used for cultic purposes.

The Mycenaean shrine (3).

View of the SE complex from the west.

The east wing of the SE complex, characterised by its double colonnades (2a, 2b).

The Neopalatial villa

The SW servants' complex

The oblong light-well (6a) in the east of the servants' rooms (6). Entrance (6b) and the magazine (6c) can be seen.

To visit the villa, which as we have said is only partially preserved due to the 'encroachment' onto it by later Mycenaean buildings, we proceed towards the medieval Church of Ayios Yeoryios Galatas, to the SW of the archaeological site. If we stop at the entrance to the church and look towards the NW, the splendid building appears to take the form of the Greek letter Γ lying on its side. At the south-west end of the villa (and indeed of the whole archaeological site) the complex of rooms **(6)** was intended as servants' quarters, as is seen from the construction, which was not particularly careful, and from the untreated floor of compacted earth. This was a series of rooms which were not intercommunicating; they were lit by windows which were situated only on the eastern side, inside a rectangular light-well **(6a)**. These were double rooms and

Light-well 6a from the south, with the characteristic built 'crypt' in its floor.

The medieval church of Ayios Yeoryios Galatas to the SW of the archaeological site.

The complex of rooms (6) which were intended as servants' quarters.

The storeroom of vessels 6d with the characteristic pillars in the middle of it.

entrance to them was probably from the west side. A paved Minoan road led from the same side in a north-south direction, a fact which gives the impression that these rooms formed a complex of workshops with immediate access to the road. There was an entrance **(6b)** at the SW end of the complex while the rooms to its east **(6c)** were storerooms containing pithoi. Room **6d** is one of the latter, notable for its two pillars in the middle and apparently used as a storeroom for vessels. We should not forget to mention that the servants' quarters 'yielded' the famous 'chieftain's cup', a stone vessel made of steatite, bearing scenes depicting a prince, an officer and three soldiers.

The NW royal apartments

Exactly north of the complex of servants' quarters, in the NW corner of the villa, there are the luxurious, **royal apartments** and their ancillary rooms **(7)**; these are evidenced immediately by the splendid paved floors with the red-grouted joints and also by the precious finds of a symbolic and cultic character such as stone vases, double axes and rhyta. Room **7a** with the alabaster orthostats in the walls has been considered to have been some kind of 'bakery', since a variety of bases has been found there in which stones with hollows in them were inserted; it has been suggested that they were used for making bread dough. The surrounding areas, which included amongst them a light-well and a

Magazine 7a with the base for the preparation of bread dough.

Room 7c with the square polythyro. In the background, rooms 7e, 7f and 7g respectively are visible.

A section of the alabaster floor in luxurious room 7c.

The fine room 7g with the alabaster orthostats and the benches around the walls.

stairway which led to the upper floor, are constructed with fine materials and were also ancillary to the royal apartments; one example is room **7b** which was a storeroom for large pithoi. The living space of the royal apartments began from the square room **7c** which is remarkable because of its alabaster orthostats and its two polythyra: one opening onto court **7d** and one onto area **7e**. Court 7d is also square; with its portico and colonnades it was orientated towards the NW, affording visitors to it a wonderful view.

The famous 'harvesters' rhyton', which was found in room 7g of the NW complex of luxurious rooms of the Neopalatial villa, depicts a procession of young Minoans. The young men with their muscular bodies are moving in a procession, singing, while a musician keeps them in step by shaking the sistrum.

We should mention here that the incomparable stone 'boxers' rhyton' was found in the portico located between room 7c and the court. We proceed from the room with the polythyra (7c)

to hall 7e which had an alabaster floor and communicated with light-well **7f**, and thereafter to room **7g** with its characteristic alabaster benches along the walls. The famous 'harvesters' rhyton' was found here; it is probable that it fell through from the upper floor when the villa was

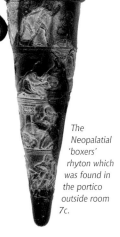

The Neopalatial 'boxers' rhyton which was found in the portico outside room 7c.

Room 7h of the NW apartments, from the north.

destroyed. The large sheet of alabaster found in the little room exactly east of 7f has been interpreted as 'a bed'.

We return to court 7d, in order to visit the fine room **7h** with its three polythyra, alabaster walls and floors. An impressive archive was found here with 450 sealstones which must also have fallen through from the floor above. The polythyro on the northern side led to a room of which nothing remains today, while that on the eastern side led to a fine, two-

The interior of room 7h.

roomed apartment with alabaster floors. Impressive frescoes were discovered in the more northerly part of the apartment; they are housed today in Heraklion Archaeological Museum. North of the area with the frescoes there was a light-well **(7i)** from which the bases of three pillars are preserved.

The north magazines

Leaving the NW corner with its fine spaces, we proceed in an easterly direction, crossing the north road. This paved road is stepped and runs in front of the north façade of the Neopalatial villa

The northern road.

which is characterised by the recesses and projections that are so typical of Minoan architecture. A large part of the north side is taken up by the magazines **(8)**, on which large-scale destruction was wrought by the building of the Mycenaean megaron above them; for this reason in most cases we are unable to discern where the entrances to them, or the doors linking them, were located. In spite of this, it is clear that the magazines were divided into two categories: those built with luxurious materials, such as alabaster floors and marble orthostats, and those which were less carefully built with earth floors. Out of the whole complex, mention should be made of room **8a** with its lined walls and alabaster floor. Although the

A Neopalatial pithos in magazine 8d of the northern complex of magazines.

The pithoi in north magazine 8d.

the long, narrow room **8e** which most probably was the location of a wooden stairway to the upper floor and east of it is magazine **8f**, where large pithoi were also found. A series of small storerooms **(8g)** occupies the eastern side of the complex; these most probably served the luxurious apartments in the NE corner of the villa. In addition to pithoi and other vessels, these yielded tablets in the Linear A script.

rectangular base of a pillar which is preserved in the middle of it previously led some researchers to believe that it constituted some kind of cultic place, it is considered certain today that it was a storeroom, given that the finds do not attest to any kind of cultic use. Exactly to the east of 8a, magazines **8b** and **8c** are notable because of their excellent construction and they were also used for the storage of vessels. Further

to the east, area **8d** provided for the storage of large Minoan pithoi, some of which bear the characteristic relief and incised decoration and are still in situ. Next is

Magazine 8a with its alabaster floor.

The NW royal apartments

The splendid NE complex

In the NE corner of the villa, east of the magazines, there is a complex of luxurious apartments **(9)** with polythyra, alabaster floors, dados, benches, and light-wells. The eastern limit of the complex was a small, terraced road which connected the north road with the southern 'Court of Shrines'. Unfortunately these splendid apartments, which are believed to have been for women, suffered great destruction during the Mycenaean period, characteristic of which is the drainage channel which is preserved in excellent condition and seems to run above the remains of the villa.

The stairway which led to the upper floor of the luxurious complex in the NE.

The entrance to the apartments was on the eastern passageway **9a** which in turn could be entered from the north, central road. This passageway ended at a stairway which led to the southern court and divided the apartments into two parts: the eastern which is notable for its large open space **9b** and the western with its residential rooms. Typical of these is room **9c** with the alabaster floor and the polythyra on its northern and southern sides. Exactly east of it there was an anteroom which led, via a portico of which the base of one pillar is preserved, to a light-well **9d**. The central space of the apartment included a large room and a portico with alabaster floors and

General view of the NE complex.

benches decorated with triglyphs and metopes. East of the complex of luxurious apartments there was an imposing stairway **(10)** which connected the north with the south court of the villa. This stairway was not connected exclusively with the luxurious apartments in the NE, but had a public character.

The stairway which led from the NE complex of royal apartments to the south court of the villa.

The NE complex of the villa and the Mycenaean drain which later passed over it.

Monumental stairway 10 which ran from the east of the splendid NE complex, connecting the north and south courts.

The splendid NE complex and part of the 'Mycenaean village

The north court, the 'bastion', the 'Mycenaean village', and the Mycenaean 'agora'

Court 11 with its characteristic stoa on the eastern side.

The north road which ran in front of the main façade of the villa arrives in the east at a court **(11)**. The latter, situated between the royal apartments and the Minoan city was closed on three sides and open only on the western side. Along the length of the eastern side there was a stoa (portico) formed by five pillars, the lower sections of which are preserved in excellent condition. A rectangular building of strong construction and on a north-south orientation **(12)** 'closed off' the northern side of the court. This building, on account of its method of construction with huge, hewn blocks, has been named 'a bastion' although its actual use remains unknown.

The NE end of the archaeological site contained a complex of Neopalatial dwellings upon which the so-called 'Mycenaean village' **(13)** was built at a later date. To the east of the village there is a large square on the right hand side of which there stood an imposing stoa constructed of columns and pillars placed alternately. At the southern end of the stoa a stairway led to the upper floor, while behind the stoa a series of eight rectangular rooms are probably to be identified as the village shops. It is worthy of note that the arrangement and the architecture of the so-called 'Mycenaean agora' **(14)** did not differ much from

General view of the NE complex.

The 'Mycenaean Agora' (14) from the north.

The stairway on the southern side of the Mycenaean agora, leading to the upper floor.

that of the much later agora of the Hellenistic period. Beyond the NE end of the archaeological site, there are the remains of two circular tombs which it is believed were vaulted tombs belonging to the 3rd millennium BC. South of these are other, later rectangular tombs, one of which contained the famous Ayia Triada sarcophagus now in Heraklion Museum. It is probable that a prominent member of the Nepalatial court was buried in this stone sarcophagus, which was decorated with scenes of a cultic nature of incomparable artistic merit.

The stone sarcophagus from Ayia Triada is decorated with scenes of a cultic nature of incomparable artistic merit.
On one side of the sarcophagus there is a scene depicting the sacrifice of animals. Accompanying the sacrifice are a flautist and some female figures, one of whom, as a priestess, makes an offering on an altar which is located in front of the 'Sacred Tree'.
On the other side, two groups are depicted moving in different directions. One group moves towards the left and consists of female figures who, accompanied by a musician playing a lyre, carry the blood from slaughtered animals and 'offer' it to a cultic vessel supported between columns topped with double axes. The other group consisting of male figures who carry animals and a model of a ship, move towards the right to offer them to an upright male figure wrapped in the fleece of an animal. It has been suggested that this figure represents the dead person and the building behind, the tomb. On the shorter sides there are depictions of chariots with two figures; in one of them, the chariot is drawn by griffons and in the other, by horses.

Remains of the tholos tomb at the NE end of the archaeological site.

The 'Mycenaean village', and the Mycenaean 'agora'

BIBLIOGRAPHY

Betancourt P., *History of Minoan Pottery*, Princeton, 1985.

Branigan K., *The Tombs of Messara*, London, 1970.

Cadogan G., *Palaces of Minoan Crete*, London, 1976.

Godart L., *The Phaistos Disc, the mystery of an Aegean script*, Athens 1995.

Graham, J.W., *The Palaces of Crete*, Princeton, 1962.

Halbherr F.- Stefani E.- Banti L., "Haghia Triada nel Periodo Tardo Palaziale", Annuario 55 [1977] (1980), 13-291.

Levi D., *Festos e la città minoica I*, Roma, 1976.

Levi D.- Carinci F., *Festos e la città minoica II*, Roma, 1988.

Myers W & E. and Cadogan G., *The Aerial Atlas of Ancient Crete*, Berkeley, 1992.

Pendlebury J.D.S., *The Archaeology of Crete: An Introduction*, London, 1939.

Pernier L., *Il palazzo minoico di Festos I*, Roma, 1935.

Pernier L. & Banti L., *Il palazzo minoico di Festos II*, Roma, 1951.

Δαβαρασ Κ., *Φαιστός, Αγία Τριάδα, Γόρτυς*, Αθήνα.

Καντα Α., *Φαιστός, Αγία Τριάδα, Γόρτυς*, Αθήνα, 1998.

Χατζη - Βαλλιανου Δ., *Φαιστός*, Αθήνα, 1989.